—LEAD|

MOUNTAINTOP MOMENTS

———

MEETING GOD IN THE HIGH PLACES

ED ROBB

by Jennifer Wilder Morgan

Abingdon Press / Nashville

Mountaintop Moments
Meeting God in the High Places
Leader Guide

ISBN 978-1-5018-8403-0

ISBN 978-1-5018-8404-7 eBook

19 20 21 22 23 24 25 26 27 28 — 10 9 8 7 6 5 4 3 2 1
MANUFACTURED IN THE UNITED STATES OF AMERICA

CONTENTS

TO THE LEADER

For the LORD is the great God,
the great King above all gods.
In his hand are the depths of the earth,
and the mountain peaks belong to him.

(Psalm 95:3-4)

Welcome to *Mountaintop Moments*, and thank you for your willingness to accompany a group of travelers into the high places of Scripture—to the mountains that carry within their peaks a revelation of God's enduring presence. Since the beginning of biblical history, mountains have played a significant role in the story of our faith. The psalmist reminds us that

From heaven the LORD looks down
and sees all mankind;
from his dwelling place he watches
all who live on earth—
he who forms the hearts of all,
who considers everything they do.

(Psalm 33:13-15)

From his high place, God has faithfully watched over the journeys of his people. He rejoiced when they walked the straight and righteous path set before them. But when their steps began to falter, God drew them aside to provide encouragement, correction, strategy, and life-giving blessings. He often drew them aside to the mountains.

In this study, we will join the children of Israel as they turn aside to answer God's summons to six different mountains in Scripture. While we stand atop each summit, our goal is to gain new perspective as we see and hear God's message—to experience the panoramic revelation that comes when we are set apart in the high places that belong to God. And with the help of the Holy Spirit, the lessons learned by the children of Israel will greatly enrich and strengthen our own personal faith journeys.

The best part of a mountaintop moment is to share the experience with others. In the tradition of auto racing, there is a phenomenon known as "bench racing," when racers, at the end of the day, sit in the paddock with their cars and fellow drivers and passionately relive every turn, near miss, and finish-line crossing. As a leader in this study, you will lead your group in a similar fashion—"base camp climbing," if you will. Under your guidance, after each ascent, your fellow climbers will reveal their personal journeys, challenges, and life-changing inspirations.

The study in this Leader Guide for Pastor Ed Robb's book, *Mountaintop Moments: Meeting God in the High Places*, will be composed of six sessions. Participants will read one chapter from the book prior to each session. The group will meet once per week for six weeks to discuss the chapter contents and selected Bible readings. At each meeting, participants will view one of six videos from the DVD, which will feature a personal mountaintop moment story relating to the chapter's content.

The sessions in the Leader Guide are designed to be completed in sixty to ninety minutes each. (Due to the amount of content provided, ninety minutes is suggested.) Suggested times for each component in a sixty-minute session are listed. If you conduct ninety-minute sessions, add time to the components as necessary.

Group discussion is a vital part of this study. Depending upon the size of your group, you may want to break participants into smaller groups to enable all participants to be involved in sharing their thoughts and ideas. The ideal group size is between six and twelve individuals. Use your own discretion.

The following is the suggested session format. But make it your own! You may choose to incorporate any or all of the activities—this plan provides options for being flexible to the needs of your group. You may choose to make take-home handouts of the questions/

activities not used during the session to enable participants to further explore chapter content on their own.

Session Planning

Each session in this Leader Guide will contain the following components:

- **Session Summary**: This summary contains the core of the chapter's teaching. The summary is for your benefit as the leader, in order to help you gather your thoughts as you plan your session. It does not need to be shared with the group unless you feel it would be beneficial. The summary consists of condensed content from the book chapter; and, at times, portions of this content will be included in the lessons.

- **Goals**: These are the insights the participants should gain by the conclusion of the session.

- **Preparation**: Make sure to read this section before each session. Preparation instructions specific to each lesson will be provided for you.

- **Session Opening** (5 mins.): Locate the session's mountain on a map and begin with a reading of the foundational Scripture, which is found at the beginning of each chapter. Ask for a volunteer to read the Scripture. Then offer up an opening prayer—use your own or the one provided.

- **Video Presentation and Discussion** (15 mins.): Show the video specific to each chapter. Pastor Ed Robb will introduce each presenter. After viewing the video, discuss the questions provided in each session, including any questions raised by participants.

- **Book Study and Discussion** (15 mins.): Begin by asking participants to share insights they gained during the week after reading the chapter. Then move to the discussion topics and related questions listed in the guide for each session.

- **Bible Study and Discussion** (15 mins.): Each session will examine a section of Scripture that is related to the core teaching of the chapter. Invite volunteers to read Scripture passages aloud (unless otherwise noted) while other participants follow along in their Bibles. Discuss the questions provided after each Scripture reading.

- **Session Closing** (10 mins.): Closing will include several brief activities—discussion of journaled insights and responses to the Peak Perspectives devotional at the end of each chapter; a hymn or other reading/activity; and the closing prayer. Before the closing prayer, ask participants to share concerns that can be prayed for by all during the week. Close with a prayer of your own or use the one provided. It is acceptable—suggested, even—that at each closing you ask for a volunteer to offer the prayer. You might not get any takers, but it is good to ask.

- **Optional Activities**: (Downloadable resource from https://www.abingdonpress.com/mountaintopmoments download) The activities provided in this section are to give you ideas and opportunities to guide participants deeper into the content of the lesson. Use your discretion as to what additional activities time will permit. The items not included during class time can be provided in a handout at the end of the session for participants to pursue on their own.

- **Cliffhanger**: (Downloadable resource from https://www .abingdonpress.com/mountaintopmomentsdownload) Each session will provide an interesting story, anecdote, or reading intended to enrich the learning experience. As time permits, this material can be presented briefly in class. Include it on a take-home handout for participants to pursue further on their own.

Tips for a Meaningful Adventure

- Prior to the initial session, reach out by email or phone to all participants and welcome them to the study. Provide a list of items to bring to each session (supplies/study tools), and provide the reading assignment to be completed before the first session. Also provide detailed instructions about where to find the classroom or meeting place. Instruct participants to journal insights from the chapter and devotional assigned each week.

- For each session, participants will need the *Mountaintop Moments* book, a Bible, and journaling material (notebook and pen or pencil).

- Before each session, familiarize yourself with the session's content. Read the session outline in this Leader Guide.

- Choose the session elements you wish to use, including the specific questions you plan to cover. Be prepared to adjust the session as participants interact and questions arise. Let the Holy Spirit move the conversation.

- Prepare the meeting space to enhance the learning process. Ideally, participants should be seated around a table or in a circle so that everyone can be included. Movable chairs are ideal so that participants can break into smaller groups for discussion.

- Most importantly, have fun with this *Mountaintop Moments* adventure and enjoy the fellowship of your fellow climbers. May God bless you on your journey!

MORIAH: MOUNT OF PROVISION

Session Summary

God began our salvation story thousands of years before the birth of Christ, when he called Abraham. Genesis chapters 11-21 teach us that Abraham was a man who was called to follow God. A man with whom God made a covenant. A man whose offspring was promised to be too numerous to count. A man who would live a life of obedience.

Abraham was called by God to be different. In essence, God was saying, "Abraham, you and your descendants are not going to live like all those other people—those tribes that surround you. You're not going to bow down before their gods and worship the way they worship."

So God called Abraham to the mountaintop at Moriah, not for him to practice human sacrifice, but to teach him that his God was different. God alone provides the sacrifice. And there's more to the great truth taught at Mount Moriah. God didn't want Abraham to give his son as an offering. God wanted Abraham to offer his own life at the altar.

What does that mean? It means not holding anything back. Giving God every part of our life—even the part that is most precious to us. It means giving God our future and trusting in his provision. So, when Abraham was called to Mount Moriah to sacrifice his son, he chose to name God's faithfulness and said in a simple but powerful profession of faith, "The Lord will provide."

We can learn an important lesson from Abraham's story—to speak boldly what we believe God has promised to do in our lives, just as Abraham did. Many of you already know firsthand the truth dramatically taught at Mount Moriah. God listens to our prayers. And God provides. In his time. In his way.

Goals

1. To understand that obedience is born of our trust in a faithful God
2. To understand that God provides for the needs of his people
3. To understand that our salvation story in Christ began four thousand years ago with a promise to Abraham

Preparation

1. Before participants arrive, pray to invite the Holy Spirit into the classroom and into your discussions.
2. Have a Bible atlas or biblical map available for use in locating Mount Moriah.
3. Have Bibles and hymnals available for participants, or have the Scriptures and/or hymns printed out on paper. If you decide to play the song from an electronic or online source, make sure it is ready to play.
4. Prepare any handouts from the online additional resources (found at https://www.abingdonpress.com /mountaintopmomentsdownload).

Session Opening (5 mins.)

1. Read the following to the participants:

Welcome to the *Mountaintop Moments* study!

To the children of Israel, high places were holy places—places where they felt close to their God. They climbed to the high places to seek God, to worship him, to learn from him, to pray to him, and to praise him. Together, we will follow in the footsteps of God's chosen people as we climb the mountains of Moriah, Sinai, Carmel, Beatitudes, Tabor, and Zion. In the ancient tradition of rabbinical teaching, we will follow our rabbi up into the high places, carrying nothing but our open minds and open hearts. Our hands must be free to help one another along the journey, for at times the climb will be steep. We will listen to the Master Storyteller as he teaches us his ways; and, like the children of Israel, we'll make use of the prayers, songs, and praises of our faith throughout the journey. May *Jehovah Shalom*—the God of Peace—be with us.

2. On a map, locate Mount Moriah (Israel) and Mount Ararat (Turkey). Note the location of Mount Moriah as it relates to Jerusalem, Solomon's Temple, and the Dome of the Rock.
3. Ask a volunteer to read the foundational Scripture at the beginning of chapter 1:

    Delight yourself in the LORD,
    *   and he will give you the desires of your heart.*

    Commit your way to the LORD;
    *   trust in him, and he will act.*

                                    (Psalm 37:4-5 ESV)

4. Open with your own prayer or use this one:

    "Come, Holy Spirit, and dwell with us in this place as we learn from your Word. Help us to reach new heights in our understanding of your love and provision for us. Know that with each step of our journey, we seek to draw ever nearer to you; in Jesus' name we pray. Amen."

Video Presentation and Discussion (15 mins.)

Watch the session video and discuss:

- Have you ever been on a mountain? If so, what was your experience? How did it change your perspective?
- In the video, Ed Robb mentions the old saying, "When you cannot trace his hand, you can always trust his heart." Have you ever followed God's instruction, even when you didn't understand where he was leading you?
- Have you ever had one of those "at the last moment" experiences when God's faithfulness and provision became very real to you? Perhaps there has been a time when you felt all hope was lost—with your finances or a personal relationship—until God intervened?

Book Study and Discussion (15 mins.)

To begin, have participants share insights they experienced as they read the chapter. Ask the question, "What perspective did you gain from the mountaintop that you couldn't see from the ground?"

Read the following, adapted from the Mountaintop Moments *book, to the group:*

> God tested Abraham. God tested his obedience. God tested his heart and tested his priorities. God tested the Israelites in the wilderness after they left Egypt. And Jesus was tested for forty days in the desert before he began his earthly ministry.

Discuss:

- How have you experienced times of testing in your own life? How did you fare in those tests?

Read the following, adapted from the Mountaintop Moments *book, to the group:*

God asked Abraham to do the impossible when he asked him to sacrifice his son, Isaac. And yet, we learn that what God really wanted was for Abraham to offer his own life at the altar—to hold nothing back—to give God every part of his life—even that which is most precious. It meant handing the future to God and trusting in his provision.

Discuss:

- Do you have a tendency to want to be in control of your life? If so, does that desire stand in the way of your trust and obedience?
- Can you give every part of your life to God? If not, why?

Read the following, adapted from the Mountaintop Moments *book, to the group:*

Our journey to Mount Moriah helps us to understand that God is trustworthy. In a miraculous moment, everything changed. Isaac was released. The ram was substituted. The burnt offering was made. And when the sacrifice was finished, Abraham named this place *Jehovah Jireh*, "The Lord Will Provide." This was not a name that reminded him of his trial but a name that proclaimed God's deliverance. Abraham wanted this altar on Mount Moriah to be remembered not for his sufferings but for God's faithfulness.

Discuss:

- Are you able to view your most difficult trials as opportunities to see God's faithfulness in your life?
- How has God demonstrated that faithfulness?

Bible Study and Discussion (15 mins.)

Have participants read the story of Abraham and Isaac on Mount Moriah in **Genesis 22:1-14.**

Discuss:

- God alone provides the sacrifice. Identify the references in this passage that may foreshadow the coming of Jesus.
- How does obedience bring blessing?

Read aloud **Genesis 12:1-3** *and* **Genesis 17:15-21**.

Discuss:

- God began our salvation story with a promise to Abraham. Identify the references in the two sections of Scripture that point to God's promise of salvation.

Read the following to the group:

> Scripture provides two separate genealogies of Jesus. In Matthew the ancestry of Jesus is traced back to Abraham. Luke, as a Gentile, presented a genealogy that took Jesus' ancestry all the way back to Adam—the origin of humankind. Jesus is referred to by the apostle Paul as "the last Adam." Listen to what he says in 1 Corinthians 15:45-48:
>
> *So it is written: "The first man Adam became a living being"; the last Adam, a life-giving spirit. The spiritual did not come first, but the natural, and after that the spiritual. The first man was of the dust of the earth; the second man is of heaven. As was the earthly man, so are those who are of the earth; and as is the heavenly man, so also are those who are of heaven.*

Compare the two genealogies of Jesus by asking volunteers to read **Matthew 1:1-17** *and* **Luke 3:23-38**.

Discuss:

- What new perspectives did you gain from Paul's statement and the two genealogies?

- Why do you think Luke took Jesus' genealogy all the way back to Adam instead of stopping with Abraham?

*Have a participant read **John 8:53-58** to the group.*

Discuss:

- As Jesus debated in the Temple, the Jews were incredulous when Jesus told them that he knew Abraham. What new perspectives did you gain from this passage?
- What early evidence do you see of a divine plan for the salvation of the world?

Session Closing (10 mins.)

1. ***Peak Perspectives devotional:*** Ask participants to share insights they have journaled from the comparison given between Mount Moriah (Abraham) and Mount Ararat (Noah).
2. ***Hymn response to the foundational Scripture:*** Read, sing, or listen together to the hymn "Great Is Thy Faithfulness" (verses 1 and 3).[1]
3. ***Prayer:*** Ask participants to share any prayer requests. You may ask for a volunteer to offer a closing prayer.

   "Jehovah Jireh, God who provides, we thank you and praise you for your unwavering faithfulness in our lives. Help us always to see your provision in the midst of our trials; and send each of us, Lord, to be channels of your faithfulness in the lives of others; in Jesus' name we pray. Amen."

SESSION 2

SINAI: MOUNT OF GOD'S LAW

Session Summary

Three thousand years ago, Moses led the Hebrew people out of the bondage of slavery under the Egyptian pharaoh. God guided and protected them as they fled through the wilderness of Egypt and gave them miraculous safe passage through the waters of the Red Sea. Three months after their escape from the pharaoh, they were drawn aside for a meeting with their God at Mount Sinai.

God orchestrated this private encounter to speak with the Israelites about things that were crucial to their survival. The Israelites were God's chosen people—a people he had set apart to be a holy nation.

However, these people did not know how to be a holy nation. They had been enslaved four hundred years to a pharaoh in an alien land that served alien gods, far from the Promised Land that God had given to them. Life had been exceedingly harsh—the pharaoh was a cruel taskmaster. And the Israelites were a discouraged people.

They had all but forgotten God. To them, the God of Abraham, Isaac, Jacob, and Joseph was more a distant memory than a present reality. His power was forgotten. His purpose was forgotten. Even after fleeing to freedom in the desert, the Israelites were more afraid of the future than they were of the past. They had no idea how to govern, protect, or provide for themselves. They wanted to go back to Egypt. Life had broken their spirit to the point they had forgotten who they were—the beloved children of God.

At Sinai, God established a new covenant with his people and gave them his Law. His Ten Commandments shaped the Israelites' relationship with God and their relationship with each other. And with the giving of the Law, the children of Israel experienced God's *prevenient grace* (grace we have not earned). It is the grace that goes before us because of the love God has for us. And it is the grace that has pursued us since the fall to sin in Eden. Because of God's great love for the Israelites—not because of anything they did—God was merciful. They had neither earned nor deserved his mercies. God hadn't forgotten them. He brought them safely out of Egypt to the foot of Mount Sinai. Then, and only then, did God give them his Law.

As the Israelites left Sinai for the Promised Land, they had a new covenant and the Law to keep them in a right and holy relationship with their God. Though they would continuously struggle to follow the Law, God's grace always went before them.

But in Jesus we have a new and everlasting covenant—the fulfillment of the Law and the saving grace of the cross. For Jesus came to do what the Law alone could not do—save us from the power of sin and death.

Goals

1. To understand how the Law governs our relationship with God and our relationship with others
2. To understand *prevenient grace* and how it acts upon our lives
3. To understand the differences between the Abrahamic, Mosaic, and New covenants

Preparation

1. Before participants arrive, pray to invite the Holy Spirit into the classroom and into your discussions.
2. Have a Bible atlas or biblical map available for use in locating Mount Sinai.
3. Have Bibles and hymnals available for participants, or have the Scriptures and/or hymns printed out on paper. If you decide to play the song from an electronic or online source, make sure it is ready to play.
4. Have large sheets of paper, pens, and sticky notes (three inch by three inch) available for this session.
5. Distribute twelve sticky note sheets, pens, and one large sheet of paper to each participant before class begins. Prepare another large sheet of paper for display with the following template, making the numbers form a "cross" with equal distance between each of them. Be sure to read ahead so that you understand how it will be used for the activity found on page 21.

1

2

5 6 7 8 9 10

3

4

6. Prepare any handouts from the online additional resources (found at https://www.abingdonpress.com /mountaintopmomentsdownload).

Session Opening (5 mins.)

1. On a map, locate Mount Sinai in Egypt, and trace the route the Israelites took during the Exodus from Egypt to Sinai, and then from Sinai to Canaan—the Promised Land. Locate Mount Nebo in Jordan.

2. Ask a volunteer to read the foundational Scripture at the beginning of chapter 2:

> *"Listen to me, my people.*
> *Hear me, Israel,*
> *for my law will be proclaimed,*
> *and my justice will become a light to the nations.*
> *My mercy and justice are coming soon.*
> *My salvation is on the way."*
>
> *(Isaiah 51:4-5 NLT)*

3. Open with your own prayer or use this one:

> *"Come, Holy Spirit, and dwell with us in this place as we learn from your Word. Write your Law upon our hearts, and open our eyes to see your ever-present grace that goes before us; in Jesus' name we pray. Amen."*

Video Presentation and Discussion (15 mins.)

Watch the session video and discuss:

- Can you remember times when God knocked on the door of your heart and invited you to draw closer into a relationship with him?
- When God dwells within us, so does his moral code. When, like Jessica, have you found yourself convicted because God's Law is written on your heart?
- Share any new insights or perspectives you gained from Jessica's story.

Book Study and Discussion (15 mins.)

To begin, have participants share insights they experienced as they read the chapter. Ask the question, "What perspective did you gain from the mountaintop that you couldn't see from the ground?"

Read the following, adapted from the Mountaintop Moments *book, to the group:*

The Ten Commandments were given to set boundaries for the children of Israel and give them a way to enter into relationship with a holy God.

The first four of the Ten Commandments contain the vertical part of the new covenant, the laws that shaped the children of Israel's relationship *with God*. God is One, and God is supreme. God cannot be expressed in material form. God's name is holy. The Sabbath—the day of rest and worship—must be safeguarded.

The next six commandments change direction and provide the horizontal part of the covenant. These are God's laws that define our relationship *with each other*, how we are to treat one another and how we are to behave. Parents are to be honored. Human life is sacred. The right of property is conserved. Sexual purity and fidelity are demanded. False and slanderous speaking about others is condemned. Coveting is wrong.

Activity

Using the sticky notes you provided, have participants write each commandment (listed below, from Exodus 20:3-17) on one sticky note while you read each one aloud. On the two remaining sticky notes, instruct them to write "Jesus" on one and "Me" on the other. Then display your template, and instruct participants to stick their Ten Commandment notes onto their large sheet of paper following the numbering on the template. Everyone should now have a large cross on their paper. Instruct participants to place their "Jesus" note at the top of the cross and their "me" note at the bottom of the cross.

1. You shall have no other gods before me.
2. You shall not make for yourself an image.
3. You shall not misuse the name of the Lord your God.
4. Remember the Sabbath day by keeping it holy.
5. Honor your father and your mother.
6. You shall not murder.
7. You shall not commit adultery.
8. You shall not steal.

9. You shall not give false testimony against your neighbor.
10. You shall not covet anything that belongs to your neighbor.

Discuss:

- What personal characteristics describe the first four commandments and our relationship with God?
- What personal characteristics describe the next six commandments and our relationships with others?
- How would you describe the way Jesus shapes God's relationship with us—you and me?

Read the following, adapted from the Mountaintop Moments *book, to the group:*

> When we break God's law, we become stained by sin. Sin separates us from God because he is holy; and like King David in the Bathsheba story, we often experience a deep sense of inadequacy when we find ourselves in God's presence.
>
> As we enter into the presence of God, we recognize our own unworthiness and become acutely aware of our sin. We realize we'll never measure up. We can't meet God's expectations. His Law is too difficult. We are too weak. With this great chasm between us and a holy God, how can we ever enter into relationship with him?
>
> The answer to that question is *grace.* When God spoke to the Israelites from Sinai, his timing was important. God gave the Law to them *after* the Exodus; after they had seen God's judgments upon Egypt, and after they experienced the Passover— saved from death by the blood of a lamb. God spoke to them after they had experienced his saving power at the Red Sea; after they escaped Egypt—guided day and night by pillars of cloud and fire—and after they had enjoyed God's mercies in the provision of manna in the wilderness and water from a rock.

Discuss:

- Why was the Law given only after the Exodus?
- Identify the signs of God's grace before he gave the Law.
- How does God's grace relate to us today, as sinners living in a fallen world?

Bible Study and Discussion (15 minutes)

Read the following to the group:

> *Prevenient grace* is defined as grace we have not earned—grace that goes before us. There are wonderful examples of this throughout Scripture; perhaps one of the best-known is the story of the prodigal son. An undeserving son insists on his inheritance, squanders it, and returns to his father penniless, begging only for the same scraps fed to his father's pigs. But upon his return home, the son was honored with a celebration and a feast. Although his father's grace was completely undeserved, this son experienced the love of his father—a love that went before him and with him throughout his story. Today we will look at another, lesser known story in Scripture about prevenient grace.
>
> Scripture tells of a five-year-old boy named Mephibosheth (Meh-fib-o-sheth), who was the son of King Saul's son, Jonathan. King Saul and his sons, including Jonathan, had been killed in a battle. Here is how this is described in 2 Samuel:
>
> *(Jonathan son of Saul had a son who was lame in both feet. He was five years old when the news about Saul and Jonathan came from Jezreel. His nurse picked him up and fled, but as she hurried to leave, he fell and became disabled. His name was Mephibosheth.)*
> *(2 Samuel 4:4)*
>
> Jonathan, son of King Saul, was King David's dearest friend. Now let's look at the rest of this story.

*Ask for a volunteer to read **2 Samuel 9:1-11**.*

Discuss:

- David's love for his friend Jonathan was the grace that went before Mephibosheth. Where in your life have you witnessed this kind of grace?
- What societal programs in our world today reflect the concept of prevenient grace?

Read the following aloud to the group; then ask volunteers to read aloud the three covenants as found in Scripture:

> Throughout biblical history, God established covenants with his people. In the Abrahamic, Mosaic, and new covenants, God made clear the depth and commitment of his relationship with humankind.

- Abrahamic covenant (Genesis 17:1-11)
- Mosaic covenant (Leviticus 26:1-4, 9-12)
- New covenant (Jeremiah 31:31-33; Luke 22:20)

Discuss:

- What were the responsibilities of the parties (God and humanity) of each covenant?

Session Closing (10 mins.)

1. ***Peak Perspectives devotional:*** Ask participants to share insights they have journaled from the comparison between Mount Sinai and Mount Nebo. Moses left a legacy in Joshua that would lead the people into the Promised Land. What legacy are you leaving for God's kingdom?
2. ***Hymn response to the foundational Scripture:*** Read, sing, or listen together to the hymn "Amazing Grace" (verses 1-4).[1]

3. **Prayer:** Ask participants to share any prayer requests. You may ask for a volunteer to offer a closing prayer.

   "God of might and God of grace, thank you for writing your law in both our minds and our hearts. Help us to live out our lives as your covenant people—faithful, thankful, and loved; in Jesus' name we pray. Amen."

CARMEL: MOUNT OF DECISION

Session Summary

We have many choices to make in life. Sometimes the choices seem easy and straightforward, and at other times the way forward is not so clear. But, at some point, our very lives will depend upon the choices we make.

Scripture records that one king after another ruled the land of Israel. The king's success, and indeed the success of the nation as a whole, depended upon the measure of the king's allegiance to God's law. In the book of 1 Kings, there is a striking downward spiral in the leadership and faithfulness of God's people. King after king did evil in the sight of the Lord, while only a handful of rulers actually followed God's law. And, for the most part, the children of Israel followed the allegiances of these kings—accommodating the seduction of pagan gods and false idols.

By the time Ahab ascended the throne, idolatry had reached such a fever pitch that worship of the one true God was barely tolerated. Worship of pagan gods was the rule in the house of Ahab and his queen, Jezebel. Sadly, a great heritage doesn't guarantee a living faith. The nation of Israel had a heritage steeped in the legacies of Abraham, Isaac, Jacob, and Joseph, and of their spiritual fathers Moses, Joshua, Samuel, and David. Turning away from God is serious business, as the children of Israel were to find out. For three years God withheld rain from the land. Without it, the people could not grow crops. Israel was hungry and miserable.

Then, at the darkest hour, when all hope seemed lost, God acted. Without warning and without introduction, the prophet Elijah burst upon the scene. He came to restore the faithful covenant relationship between the people of Israel and their God. In a mighty showdown on top of Mount Carmel, Elijah summoned the children of Israel, along with the prophets of Baal and Asherah, who were loyal to Ahab and Jezebel.

> Elijah went before the people and said, "How long will you waver between two opinions? If the LORD is God, follow him; but if Baal is God, follow him."
>
> But the people said nothing.
>
> (1 Kings 18:21)

They couldn't decide. The remainder of the narrative in 1 Kings 18 tells the compelling story of God's victory over the prophets of Baal by sending fire down from heaven at Elijah's request. This fire reignited the flames of faith in the hearts of God's chosen people.

From the burning bush to the pillars of fire in the wilderness, from the fiery cloud on Sinai to the flames of Elijah's altar on Mount Carmel, the holy fire of God has served as a mighty beacon, lighting the way for those with the courage and faith to choose the narrow road. Today God shines his mighty light on the road we all must travel—the road that leads to Calvary.

Goals

1. To understand that apostasy—falling away from God—is gradual
2. To understand that our eternal future depends not on our spiritual heritage but on the personal choices we make

3. To understand that as human beings we are fragile, but God is greater than our fears and trials

Preparation

1. Before participants arrive, pray to invite the Holy Spirit into the classroom and into your discussions.
2. Have a Bible atlas or biblical map available for use in locating Mount Carmel.
3. Have Bibles and hymnals available for participants, or have the Scriptures and/or hymns printed out on paper. If you decide to play the song from an electronic or online source, make sure it is ready to play.
4. Prepare any handouts from the online additional resources (found at https://www.abingdonpress.com /mountaintopmomentsdownload).

Session Opening (5 mins.)

1. On a map, locate Mount Carmel. Search online for photos of Mount Carmel as it is today, and view the striking statue of the victorious prophet Elijah that stands in the courtyard of the Carmelite monastery atop Mount Carmel.
2. Ask a volunteer to read the foundational Scripture at the beginning of chapter 3:

   "Enter through the narrow gate. For wide is the gate and broad is the road that leads to destruction, and many enter through it. But small is the gate and narrow the road that leads to life, and only a few find it."
   (Matthew 7:13-14)

3. Open with your own prayer or use this one:

   "Come Holy Spirit, and dwell with us in this place as we learn from your Word. As we meet you with Elijah on Mount Carmel, let the fire of your Spirit awaken our hearts and rekindle the flames of our faith; in Jesus' name we pray. Amen."

Video Presentation and Discussion (15 mins.)

Watch the session video and discuss:

- How has God proved himself and his sovereignty to you?
- Do you have the confidence of Elijah to see you through difficult decisions?
- What is the condition of your relationship with God today?

Book Study and Discussion (15 mins.)

To begin, have participants share insights they experienced as they read the chapter. Ask the question, "What perspective did you gain from the mountaintop that you couldn't see from the ground?"

Read the following, summarized from the Mountaintop Moments *book, to the group:*

> Israel's slide into apostasy was gradual. For thousands of years, the Hebrew people had lived surrounded by nations who worshiped visible gods, idols you could see and touch; they were alluring gods who spoke to the desires of the flesh—power, money, sex, and prestige. The kings of Israel began to accept the worship of gods other than Jehovah, and the people followed in step with their kings. These visible gods were popular with the people and didn't make so many demands, so the Israelites embraced the well-trodden path of pagan worship.

Discuss:

- Israel's King Hezekiah was a faithful king who did right in the eyes of God. In the wake of the Assyrian king's mockery of Israel's God, Hezekiah offered a heartfelt prayer begging God for deliverance, found in **2 Kings 19:14-19**. *Have a volunteer read this to the group.*
- If you were a modern-day Hezekiah, how would your prayer sound? What do the idols shaped by human

29

hands look like today? Where can we place our hope for deliverance?

- Just as a nation can slide into apostasy, so also can individuals. Have there been times in your life when you have fallen away from God? What caused that? How did you return to God?

Read the following, adapted from the Mountaintop Moments *book, to the group:*

> One thing we do know about Elijah is that his conviction and courage cause him to stand out as one of the great heroes of the Hebrew people. Why is this prophet so revered? It's because at a critical moment in Israel's history he stood firm for monotheism. When all the cultural tides were against him, Elijah fought against syncretism (the combination of different forms of belief and practice), summoning the courage to defy the king of Israel and challenge the ones Scripture calls "the false prophets of Baal." Elijah fought for God, and he fought for the faith of his people.

Discuss:

- When have you been called to defend your faith? to encourage others in their faith?

Bible Study and Discussion (15 mins.)

Read the following, adapted from the Mountaintop Moments *book, to the group:*

> After God's impressive defeat of Baal on Mount Carmel, *Elijah slid into despair.* When King Ahab told Queen Jezebel everything Elijah had done, and how he had killed all the prophets with the sword, Jezebel sent a messenger to Elijah with her threat: "The gods will get you for this and I'll get even with you! By this time tomorrow you'll be as dead as any one of those prophets" (1 Kings 19:2 MSG).

Then say:

> Let's look at what happened next with Elijah and with
> two other figures from Scripture.

Ask a volunteer to read aloud **Genesis 21:14-20**; **1 Kings 19:3-5**; *and*
Matthew 4:1-11.

Discuss:

- All three of these stories reflect God's care and provision of
  people who were afraid, desperate, exhausted, and tested.
  Discuss the way God ministered in each of these situations.
- How has God ministered to you in times of trial?

Read the following to the group:

> The choice to follow God is a central theme through-
> out both the Old and New Testaments. It is a choice
> that has eternal consequences. Listen to the following
> sections of Scripture, paying attention to the choice
> of the people and the consequences of their choice.

Ask a volunteer to read aloud **Joshua 24:14-15, 23-27.**

Discuss:

- What was the choice of the people once they reached the
  Promised Land? What was the consequence?

Ask a volunteer to read aloud **Ruth 1:3-5, 7-8, 16-19,** *and* **4:18-22.**

Then read the following to the group:

> Ruth, originally from Moab, was the grandmother of
> King David. (Ruth married Boaz. Their son, Obed,
> was the father of Jesse. Jesse was the father of King
> David.)

"Praise the Lord, all you Gentiles;
*   let all the peoples extol him."*

And again, Isaiah says,

"The Root of Jesse will spring up,
*   one who will arise to rule over the nations;*
*   in him the Gentiles will hope."*

May the God of hope fill you with all joy and peace
as you trust in him, so that you may overflow with
hope by the power of the Holy Spirit.
*   (Romans 15:11-13)*

Discuss:

- Jesus is the branch that springs up from the root of Jesse. With this in mind, what was Ruth's choice, and what were the consequences of her choice?
- In today's world, what are the consequences of your choice to follow Jesus?

Session Closing (10 mins.)

1. **Peak Perspectives devotional:** Ask participants to share insights they have journaled from the comparison given between Mount Carmel and the mountain of Masada.
2. **Hymn response to the foundational Scripture:** Read, sing, or listen together to the hymn "Trust and Obey" (verses 1 and 4).[1]
3. **Prayer:** Ask participants to share any prayer requests. You may ask for a volunteer to offer a closing prayer.

"'Hear, O Israel: the Lord our God, the Lord is one. Love
the Lord your God with all your heart and with all your
soul and with all your strength.' Write these words
upon our hearts, holy Father, so we can walk in eternal
fellowship with you; in Jesus' name we pray. Amen."

SESSION 4

BEATITUDES: MOUNT OF BLESSINGS

Session Summary

As we step into the New Testament, we cross a theological divide—the life and ministry of Jesus Christ. His preaching was not like the other rabbis'. He taught as one who had authority, and the people who heard him were amazed. Crowds would gather on the hillsides, eager to hear Jesus' teachings and receive the gift of his healings. Jesus' disciple Matthew describes these hillside ministry moments in a compilation of teachings called the Sermon on the Mount.

As Jesus began to deliver his Sermon on the Mount, his listeners—disciples, admirers, and scoffers—were about to have an otherworldly experience. He drew aside the curtain of the heavenly realm, providing his listeners with a glimpse into an unseen Kingdom. In the person of Jesus Christ, a new world had planted itself in their midst—a world they would discover to be far different from their own—a world Jesus insisted would be their future. This world was the kingdom of heaven—the same kingdom that Jesus proclaimed to have *"come near."*

These teachings of Jesus were difficult for his listeners to understand. They seemed completely contrary—upside down—to the world in which they lived. Actually, he was turning the world of his listeners right-side up. With his delivery of the Sermon on the Mount, Jesus Christ presented the first-century people of Israel with an astonishing look at a new world, a new way of life, and a mighty choice to make. Which world would they belong to?

The question remains the same for us today. Will we choose to continue to belong to a world of selfishness, persecution, retaliation, and death? Or will we choose to belong to a world of mercy, compassion, holiness, and eternal life? We are invited to live otherworldly lives in a desperately fallen world with a relentless calling.

Jesus' teachings reveal that the way into the Kingdom is challenging. The gate is narrow. A change of heart is necessary and so is childlike faith. The requirements are as difficult as the Mount of Beatitudes is steep. On this mountain Jesus drew a dividing line between the world of man and the kingdom of heaven. He clearly invited all people to follow him into a new way of living. He also made it clear that the only way to enter the kingdom of heaven is through him.

Goals

1. To understand the requirements of living a Kingdom life
2. To understand the blessing Jesus brings as the spirit of God's law
3. To understand the concept of repentance and making a turnaround in thought and action

Preparation

1. Before participants arrive, pray to invite the Holy Spirit into the classroom and into your discussions.
2. Have a Bible atlas or map available for use in locating the Mount of Beatitudes and locations of Jesus' ministry in the region of the Sea of Galilee.

3. Have Bibles and hymnals available for participants, or have the Scriptures and/or hymns printed out on paper. If you decide to play the song from an electronic or online source, make sure it is ready to play.
4. For this session, you will need to prepare the following handouts: #1: Beatitudes, NIV translation; #2: Beatitudes, MSG translation; #3: Ten Commandments, MSG translation; and any handouts from the online additional resources (found at https://www.abingdonpress.com/mountaintopmomentsdownload).

Session Opening (5 mins.)

1. Locate the Mount of Beatitudes on a map. Trace the area of Jesus' ministry around the region of the Sea of Galilee and the Mount of Beatitudes.
2. Ask a volunteer to read the foundational Scripture at the beginning of chapter 4:

When Jesus heard that John had been put in prison, he withdrew to Galilee. Leaving Nazareth, he went and lived in Capernaum, which was by the lake . . . to fulfill what was said through the prophet Isaiah . . .

> *"the people living in darkness*
> *have seen a great light;*
> *on those living in the land of the shadow of death*
> *a light has dawned."*

From that time on Jesus began to preach, "Repent, for the kingdom of heaven has come near."
(Matthew 4:12-17)

3. Open with your own prayer or use this one:

"Come, Holy Spirit, and dwell with us in this place as we learn from your Word. Teach us in the way of right living, so that we may truly understand what it means when we pray, 'Your kingdom come, your will be done, on earth as it is in heaven'; in Jesus' name we pray. Amen."

Video Presentation and Discussion (15 mins.)

Watch the session video and discuss:

- Have you ever had a mountaintop experience, as Bishop Hayes describes? If you did, how did it feel? Where was it?
- How did Jesus give his listeners on the mountain a clearer picture of who he really was?
- What new perspective on the Beatitudes did you gain from this presentation?

Book Study and Discussion (15 mins.)

To begin, have participants share insights they experienced as they read the chapter. Ask the question, "What perspective did you gain from the mountaintop that you couldn't see from the ground?"

In this lesson, the class will read and discuss the Beatitudes using two different translations (provided on handouts #1 and #2).

Read the following, adapted from the Mountaintop Moments *book, to the group:*

> As Jesus began to deliver his Sermon on the Mount, his listeners—disciples, admirers, and scoffers—were about to have an otherworldly experience. In the person of Jesus Christ a new world had planted itself in their midst—a world they would discover to be far different from their own—a world Jesus insisted would be their future. This world was the kingdom of heaven—the same kingdom that Jesus proclaimed to have "come near." As the crowds pressed in around him, he opened his sermon with a curious series of blessings, which we know as the Beatitudes.

Distribute the handouts that provide the text of the Beatitudes "Blessings" (Matthew 5:3-12) in the NIV and The Message versions. Ask for volunteers to read aloud each of the "blessings," first in the NIV, followed by the same one in The Message.

Discuss:

- Think about people (religious figures, famous people) or fictional characters from books or movies whose lives reflect the characteristics of the Blessings. Which of the Beatitudes did their lives reflect?
- Describe the ways that Jesus embodies each of the Blessings.
- Consider how you—as a participant—reflect the requirements of the Blessings. Where do you meet them? Where do you not meet them?

Read the following, adapted from the Mountaintop Moments *book, to the group:*

> Following the Beatitudes Jesus presented six contrasts between the traditional teachings of the Torah and the new teachings of the kingdom of heaven. Six times, beginning with murder and ending with love for your enemies, he opened with the statement, "You have heard that it was said" and quoted the teaching of the Jewish law. And six times, he exclaimed, "But I tell you. . . ." The explanation that followed showed how the old way is not enough, and it reveals the spirit of the law. Jesus offered a more exacting standard of righteousness and challenged people to a new way of living—Kingdom living.

Have participants take turns reading aloud the following statements of Jesus found in **Matthew 5***:*

- Verse 17
- Verses 21-22
- Verses 27-28
- Verses 31-32
- Verses 38-40
- Verses 43-45
- Verse 48

*Now read to the class the apostle Paul's description of the fruit of the Spirit in **Galatians 5:22-23**.*

Discuss:

- Discuss the significance of the fruit of the Spirit and how this passage relates to Jesus' "You have heard it said" statements.

Bible Study and Discussion (15 mins.)

In this lesson the class will compare the words spoken by God in the Ten Commandments with the Beatitude blessings spoken by Jesus, with the objective of gaining further perspective on how Jesus embodies the spirit of God's law.

Refer the group to

- *Handout #1, "The Beatitudes (NIV)"*
- *Handout #3, "The Ten Commandments"*

Discuss:

- What impact does it have on you to read the commandments and then the blessings—the promises— that Jesus offers?
- With the perspective of promise or blessing in mind, review the Ten Commandments again. Describe the promise or blessing that can be obtained in each commandment if it is followed.

Read the following to the group:

> As Jesus began his ministry, he called people to repentance. The word *repent* means "to express regret or remorse for one's actions." It also means to turn around—to turn from sin—to change direction in actions and thinking. God's call to repentance is a consistent theme throughout the Old and New Testaments. Jesus' teaching on the Mount of

Beatitudes provides a look at how a change in actions and thinking can activate the kingdom of heaven on earth.

Ask volunteers to read aloud the following calls to repentance:

- Joel 2:13
- Proverbs 1:23
- Zechariah 1:3b
- 2 Peter 3:9
- Matthew 3:8
- 2 Chronicles 7:14
- Ezekiel 18:32

Discuss:

- What blessing is to be found in each call to repentance?

Read the following to the group:

When people live a repentant life, they live a changed life. Repentance is a powerful way to bring the kingdom of God into the world of humanity—to make a reality of the prayer Jesus taught us to pray, "Your will be done, on earth as it is in heaven" (Matthew 6:10).

*Have participants read **Acts 9:1-19**, in which Jesus "turned around" one of his most persistent enemies, Saul.*

Discuss:

- What was the impact Saul's conversion had on the world?
- Have you experienced the blessing of conversion and repentance? When and how? What are you doing for the Kingdom with your changed life?

Session Closing (10 mins.)

1. **Peak Perspectives devotional:** Ask participants to share insights they have journaled from the comparison given between the Mount of Beatitudes and the Mount of Olives.

2. *Hymn response to the foundational Scripture:* Read, sing, or listen together to the hymn "I Surrender All"[1] (all verses).

3. *Prayer:* Ask participants to share any prayer requests. You may ask for a volunteer to offer a closing prayer.

   "Dearest Lord Jesus, we thank you for showing us the blessings of Kingdom living. Help us to always hear your call to repentance so that we may keep our hearts, thoughts, and actions turned toward you; in your precious name we pray. Amen."

SESSION 5

TABOR: MOUNT OF TRANSFIGURATION

Session Summary

As Jesus neared the end of his earthly ministry, he took his disciples on a long and curious side trip—a retreat to the Grotto of Pan at Caesarea Philippi. The disciples must have been absolutely shocked. This was an unholy place; it was the location of a mammoth cave and temple dedicated to the worship of the pagan god Pan. The cave was known to the people of Jesus' time as a gate of Hades.

Matthew 16:13-19 tells us that as Jesus stood near this pagan temple, he asked his disciples, "Who do you say I am?" (verse 15). Simon Peter answered, "You are the Messiah, the Son of the living God" (verse 16).

That moment was a critical teaching moment for Jesus. Upon Peter's admission, Jesus gave his disciples a look at the future of their ministry: "On this rock I will build my church, and the gates of Hades will not overcome it" (verse 18). As Jesus stood before the looming, dark cave, he knew his disciples faced a lifetime of facing

41

down death and darkness with the good news of the gospel—soon to be revealed in his suffering, death, and resurrection. Upon the rock of Peter's faith, Jesus was commissioning his disciples to be the force of life against death and to establish the church everywhere they could.

Six days later, Jesus took his inner circle—Peter, James, and John—to a high place for prayer. This place was Mount Tabor, a small mountain rising abruptly from the surrounding flat plains, eleven miles west of the Sea of Galilee. What follows is one of the most unusual and breathtaking experiences recorded in the Gospel accounts; recorded not just once, but three times, in the Gospels of Matthew, Mark, and Luke—the transfiguration of Jesus.

Why did Jesus take this time away from his mission? *Because his disciples needed it.* They needed to know that all he had been teaching them about himself was true. They needed a glimpse of the victorious Christ. This was a transforming event for these three disciples. In a spectacular moment, they saw Jesus in his glory—the glory he had with God before the world began (John 17:5). Finally, the disciples began to comprehend the enormity of who Jesus was. Peter's first admission at Caesarea Philippi that Jesus was the Messiah, the Son of the living God, was an admission based on faith. Now, on Mount Tabor, Peter, James, and John were eyewitnesses to a stunning truth. Jesus was indeed the Messiah, the One sent by God to redeem Israel and this fallen world.

Goals

1. To understand transformation in both spiritual and personal contexts
2. To understand that as the bearer of the new covenant, Jesus has been given all authority in heaven and on earth
3. To understand that the power of witness is essential to the Christian faith

Preparation

1. Before participants arrive, pray to invite the Holy Spirit into the classroom and into your discussions.
2. Have a Bible atlas or biblical map available for use in locating Caesarea Philippi and Mount Tabor.

3. Have Bibles and hymnals available for participants, or have the Scriptures and/or hymns printed out on paper.
4. For the first activity in the Book Study and Discussion, you will need one bucket (be creative). You will also need a supply of index cards—one for each participant.
5. Prepare any handouts from the online additional resources (found at https://www.abingdonpress.com /mountaintopmomentsdownload).

Session Opening (5 mins.)

1. Locate Caesarea Philippi and Mount Tabor on a map.
2. Ask a volunteer to read the foundational Scripture at the beginning of chapter 5:

All your works praise you, LORD;
your faithful people extol you.
They tell of the glory of your kingdom
and speak of your might,
so that all people may know of your mighty acts
and the glorious splendor of your kingdom.
(Psalm 145:10-12)

3. Open with your own prayer or use this one:

"Come, Holy Spirit, and dwell with us in this place as we learn from your Word. Fill us with wonder, fill us with knowledge, and fill us with the passion and confidence to speak the truth about Jesus into our world today; in Jesus' name we pray. Amen."

Video Presentation and Discussion (15 mins.)

Watch the session video and discuss:

- How has your faith been influenced by the faith of others? Have you ever had to lean on someone's faith? Have you been the source of strength and faith for someone else?
- Can you change your perspective on reality as Dr. Hill suggests? When have you experienced glimpses of the eternal reality? How has that carried over into your daily life?

- Have you ever experienced a mountaintop moment as striking as the one the disciples experienced on Mount Tabor? How did it affect you?

Book Study and Discussion (15 minutes)

To begin, have participants share insights they experienced as they read the chapter. Ask the question, "What perspective did you gain from the mountaintop that you couldn't see from the ground?"

Activity

Spiritual "Bucket List"

Supplies needed: a bucket and index cards

Distribute an index card to all participants and ask them to write down what is on their own spiritual bucket list. If they need inspiration, ask:

Whom would you like to meet?
What would you like to see?
Where would you like to go?
. . . And why?"

After a few minutes when all have had a chance to complete the assignment, have each person come up, share what he or she has written, and place the index card in the bucket.

When everyone has placed their lists in the bucket, pray over the bucket, asking God that these dreams of his sons and daughters be realized—in earthly life or in eternal life. (You may ask for a volunteer to pray.)

Read the following, adapted from the Mountaintop Moments *book, to the group:*

As Jesus neared the end of his earthly ministry, he took his disciples on a long and curious side trip—a retreat to the Grotto of Pan at Caesarea Philippi. The disciples must have been absolutely shocked. This was an unholy place; it was a "sin" city in every sense of the word. This visit certainly was *not* on their bucket lists. But this was a critical teaching moment for Jesus. The cross was looming over him, and he knew the time had come for his disciples to fully understand the message he had been preaching. He asked his disciples,

"But what about you?" . . . "Who do you say I am?"

Simon Peter answered, "You are the Messiah, the Son of the living God."

Jesus replied, "Blessed are you, Simon son of Jonah, for this was not revealed to you by flesh and blood, but by my Father in heaven. And I tell you that you are Peter, and on this rock I will build my church, and the gates of Hades will not overcome it."

(Matthew 16:15-18)

Discuss:

In the time of Jesus, cities were fortified by a single gate, which permitted entry into and exit from the city. The mammoth cave located at the Grotto of Pan was believed to be a gate of Hades (hell) which forever held the deceased in the realm of death.

- With this in mind, discuss what Jesus was revealing to his disciples.

Read the passage from Luke and then read the following passage, adapted from the Mountaintop Moments *book, to the group:*

Two men, Moses and Elijah, appeared in glorious splendor, talking with Jesus. They spoke about his departure, which he was about to bring to fulfillment at Jerusalem.

(Luke 9:30-31)

Moses, the one in whom God established his covenant of the Law, and Elijah, the prophet who restored God's covenant with Israel, were discussing Jesus' *departure*. In Greek, this word is *exodos*. The first Moses, who led God's people out of slavery into freedom, was speaking about the next exodus with the *new* Moses—Jesus. Jesus was the bringer of the new covenant—the one who would lead God's people from death to life, from sin to redemption. Elijah and Moses were present to help prepare Jesus for his final exodus and return to glory.

Then, "a bright cloud covered them, and a voice from the cloud said, 'This is my Son, whom I love; with him I am well pleased. Listen to him!'" (Matthew 17:5). The disciples also knew these words from Moses' prophecy about Jesus as recorded in Deuteronomy 18:15: "The LORD your God will raise up for you a prophet like me from among you, from your fellow Israelites. You must listen to him."

When the disciples heard this, they fell facedown to the ground, terrified. But Jesus came and touched them. "Get up," he said. "Don't be afraid." When they looked up, they saw no one except Jesus.

(Matthew 17:6-8)

Discuss:

- Discuss the significance of God's command on the mountain during the transfiguration and the significance of Moses' command included in his prophecy about Jesus. Place emphasis on the word "him."
- What do you find significant about the fact that after God spoke, Moses and Elijah disappeared from sight?

Bible Study and Discussion (15 minutes)

Read the following to the group:

The word transfiguration is a derivative of the Greek word, *metamorphoo*, which means "to change into another form, to transfer, to transfigure."[1] We commonly associate the word "metamorphosis" with the dramatic change a lowly caterpillar undergoes to become a magnificent butterfly. For the caterpillar, this is a once-in-a-life-time transformation. But, in Jesus, we gain a fresh new perspective on the process of metamorphosis.

Ask volunteers to read aloud the following Scriptures, while the rest of the class listens to the readings with eyes closed. Allow a few moments after each reading for listeners to write down what they experienced with their senses as they listened (what they felt, heard, saw, tasted, touched, and so forth).

- First Reading: Luke 1:26-33, 39-44; 2:8-16
- Second Reading: Matthew 17:1-9
- Third Reading: Matthew 28:1-10; Mark 15:33-39; John 17:1-5

Discuss:

Take a few moments to let participants share their responses as they listened to the Scripture readings.

- The three readings are examples of three transfigurations— or metamorphoses—of Jesus. How did Jesus transform in each of the three readings? How are these transformations alike? How are they different?
- Jesus' broken body in the grave was resurrected and restored to a glorified body. What does this say about the possibilities of our own personal transformations?

Read the following to the group:

The power of witness is a crucial component in our belief system. Just before Peter was martyred in AD 67, he wrote a letter to the church as a reminder of the truth of Christianity, as opposed to the heresies of false teachers. In it he states,

47

For we did not follow cleverly devised stories when we told you about the coming of our Lord Jesus Christ in power, but we were eyewitnesses of his majesty. He received honor and glory from God the Father when the voice came to him from the Majestic Glory, saying, "This is my Son, whom I love; with him I am well pleased." We ourselves heard this voice that came from heaven when we were with him on the sacred mountain.

(2 Peter 1:16-18)

And John wrote this about Jesus:

The Word became flesh and made his dwelling among us. We have seen his glory, the glory of the one and only Son, who came from the Father, full of grace and truth.

(John 1:14)

These disciples carried with them the revelation of Jesus' transfiguration throughout their lives, and the written word of their testimony has encouraged believers throughout the ages. To be an eyewitness to a miraculous event is both powerful and empowering. But Scripture reminds us that believing *without* seeing is even more important.

Read the following Scriptures aloud and ask this question after each one: "What is the blessing to be found in believing what we cannot see?"

- John 20:24-29
- Romans 10:8-17
- 2 Corinthians 4:16-18

Read the following to the group:

Jesus appeared to many people between his resur-rection and ascension and encouraged their belief in him. Luke shares a compelling account of Jesus' encounter with several of his followers while walking on the road to Emmaus.

*Read Luke's account (found in **Luke 24:13-32**) aloud to the class from The Message translation.*

Discuss:

- What did Jesus do for these people he met on the road to Emmaus?
- Have you ever had the opportunity to transform the faith of one who was discouraged? How did you do that?
- Have you ever attended The Walk to Emmaus? If so, how did this experience transform your faith? (*Leader: You may choose to provide a description of The Walk to Emmaus and encourage class members to consider attending an upcoming Walk.*[2])

Session Closing (10 minutes)

1. **Peak Perspectives devotional:** Ask participants to share insights they have journaled from the comparison given between Mount Tabor and the Mount of Calvary.
2. **Collective response to the foundational Scripture:** For this lesson, the class will recite together the Apostles' Creed.[3]
3. **Prayer:** Ask participants to share any prayer requests. You may ask for a volunteer to offer a closing prayer.

    "God of Glory, power and might, thank you for revealing yourself to us in the One who lived among us. Your only Son, Jesus the Christ, came to earth to reveal to us our true reality—eternal life with you in the realm of glory. Thanks be to God! In Jesus' name we pray. Amen."

ZION: MOUNT OF GOD'S PRESENCE

Session Summary

Today, as we set out on our final journey, we turn our faces to the east and join our voices with the children of Israel in joyful songs of praise. We are making a pilgrimage to the holiest place on earth—the mount of God's presence. We are heading to *Zion*.

For the people of Israel, Mount Zion represents the place of God's presence. It's not so much the physicality of the place, but the *spirituality* of the place that has such great meaning. God doesn't reside exclusively in the Temple, nor in a shrine nor on an altar. No. More than anyone, the Hebrew people have understood the omnipresence of God's nature.

Zion is the place where King David established his fortress and where he placed the Ten Commandments given to Moses on Sinai. It is the place where David's son King Solomon built the first temple. Mount Zion is indeed a holy place—God's chosen dwelling place. It is the place where the children of Israel *connect* with Yahweh—the God of Abraham, Isaac, and Jacob.

The Israelites understood a deeper truth as well. God had a heart for his people. That connection started a long time ago. From the moment Adam and Eve fled Eden, God pursued the children he desperately loved. Throughout the centuries, God went behind them, went before them, and drew alongside them, calling them back into relationship with him. Calling them into covenant—a binding relationship that will last forever, just as it was always meant to be. This is why the children of Israel love Zion. God chose to make his dwelling place there with them. For them, Mount Zion represents the *heart* of God's presence.

Two thousand years ago, the Scriptures tell us, something truly wondrous took place in the land of Zion. The omnipresent God of Abraham, Isaac, and Jacob put on the sandals of an itinerant rabbi and walked among his beloved children of Israel for thirty-three years. He laughed with them, wept with them, broke bread with them, taught them, healed them, and loved them. The presence of God, in the person of Jesus, had become intimately *personal*.

Mount Zion embodies the spiritual presence of God on earth. Jerusalem was, is, and always shall be God's beloved city. For both the people of Israel and followers of Christ, Jerusalem is holy ground. It's the connection point of our faith. It's why we are drawn to it. It's why so many believers want to set foot in the Holy Land at least once in their lifetime.

Goals

1. To understand how we remember the presence of God in our lives
2. To understand the requirements of being a people set apart
3. To understand the concept of being a "living stone"

Preparation

1. Before participants arrive, pray to invite the Holy Spirit into the classroom and into your discussions.
2. Have a Bible atlas or biblical map available for use in locating Jerusalem and the surrounding areas—Mount Zion, Mount Moriah, the City of David, Solomon's Temple, and the Temple Mount/Dome of the Rock.

3. Have Bibles and hymnals available for participants or have the Scriptures and/or hymns printed out on paper. If you decide to play the song from an electronic or online source, make sure it is ready to play.

4. If a chalkboard or dry erase board is not available in the meeting room, have a large sheet of paper available to record the attributes of holy living (see the Bible Study and Discussion portion of the session).

5. For this lesson, you will need to make arrangements with a pastor to conduct a service of Holy Communion during the session's closing. Bread and grape juice for the sacrament will need to be provided—the pastor's office should guide you on what will be needed. If your group meeting is held in a church building, you may choose to either move to a chapel or sanctuary location, or stay in your classroom.

6. Prepare any handouts from the online additional resources (found at https://www.abingdonpress.com /mountaintopmomentsdownload).

Session Opening (5 mins.)

1. On a map, locate Jerusalem and the surrounding areas— Mount Zion, Mount Moriah, the City of David, Solomon's Temple, and the Temple Mount/Dome of the Rock.

2. Ask a volunteer to read the foundational Scripture at the beginning of chapter 6:

"Do not come any closer," God said. "Take off your sandals, for the place where you are standing is holy ground." Then he said, "I am the God of your father, the God of Abraham, the God of Isaac and the God of Jacob."

(Exodus 3:5-6)

3. Open with your own prayer or use this one:

"Come, Holy Spirit, and dwell with us in this place as we learn from your Word. Bring us into a deeper understanding of how we can connect with your presence in our daily lives and what it means to be

the holy people of a holy God; in Jesus' name we pray. Amen."

Video Presentation and Discussion (15 mins.)

Watch the session video and discuss:

- Have you ever experienced a personal encounter with God? If so, how did it change you?
- Has there been a moment, a pilgrimage, or a gift that connected you to God in a way that you will never forget?
- How have you been able to find God in the lowest moments of your life?

Book Study and Discussion (15 mins.)

To begin, have participants share insights they experienced as they read the chapter. Ask the question, "What perspective did you gain from the mountaintop that you couldn't see from the ground?"

Read the following, adapted from the Mountaintop Moments *book, to the group:*

> For the people of Israel, Zion is where they connect with Yahweh—the God of Abraham, Isaac, and Jacob. It represents the place of God's presence. It's not so much the physicality of the place, but the *spirituality* of the place that has such great meaning. God doesn't reside exclusively in the Temple, nor in a shrine nor on an altar. No. More than anyone, the Hebrew people have understood the omnipresence of God's nature. Limited by neither time nor space, *God was everywhere the Israelites went.* He spoke from a mountainside thicket to Abraham and Isaac, and he called to Moses from a burning bush. His hand delivered the plagues of Egypt, stirred the pillar of fire in the wilderness, parted the Red Sea, and provided manna and water in the desert. God went before his people into the Promised Land. He

poured down his fire upon an altar on Mount Carmel and spoke to the disciples from a bright cloud on Mount Tabor. *Everywhere the Israelites went, they discovered God was with them.* Israel's beloved King David, a man of poetry and war, knew this to be an absolute truth. Half of the 150 psalms are attributed to David, and he wrote extensively about the omnipresence of God.

Activity

For this lesson, class participants will write psalms of their own about the presence of God in their lives.

Depending on class size, break the class into several small groups. Instruct groups to work together to compose a seven-line psalm of praise for the ways they experience God's presence. (If they need ideas, you may offer subjects to consider, such as family, fellowship, worship, nature, and so forth.)

Discuss:

When the assignment has been completed by all groups, have a representative from each group read their psalm to the class.

Then all come back together and discuss the following question:

- Did you experience new insights into the omnipresence of God in this exercise? What new perspective did you gain?

Next, have a volunteer read **Psalm 139:7-12** *to the group. After the passage is read, ask:*

- How might these words from King David's psalm encourage you?

Read the following, adapted from the Mountaintop Moments *book, to the group:*

The ark of the covenant was an extravagantly decorated box; but more than that, it contained items that were greatly revered by the Hebrew people: the tablets of stone on which the Ten Commandments were inscribed; Aaron's rod, the staff of Moses' brother and high priest that demonstrated miraculous powers during the plagues of Egypt; and a jar that contained manna from the desert. The ark of the covenant was sacred to the people of Israel—its contents represented the holy, covenantal presence of God. So they carried the ark with them wherever they went. They carried it all during the forty years of wandering in the desert. Whenever they camped, the ark was placed in a special and sacred tent, called the Tabernacle. And when the Israelites crossed the Jordan River into the Promised Land, they carried the ark in front of them.

King David brought the ark of the covenant to Mount Zion, since the ark represented God's presence in the midst of his people. It reminded them of God's great acts of salvation, the Law given to Moses, God's provision during the wilderness years, and God's protection as they took possession of the Promised Land.

Continue reading out loud:

As covenantal people, we, too, want to be reminded of our connection to our God and his great acts of mercy, grace and salvation. In this lesson we will look at three of the sacraments celebrated in the Christian faith—sacraments that serve as a remembrance of this divine connection.

The first is the **Sacrament of Baptism**: an outward act that symbolizes membership in the family of God and an inward commitment to Jesus Christ. Baptism is the first step in Christian discipleship. (*Note: The Catholic Church recognizes seven sacraments, while the UMC officially recognizes only two: baptism and Communion.*)

*Have participants read **Acts 8:26-39**.*

Discuss:

- Describe the actions Philip took to bring the eunuch into baptism.
- Remember your own baptism. When was it done and how? What did this event mean to you—or your parents/family?

Continue reading out loud:

> The next sacrament is **Holy Communion**, the breaking of bread together when we remember the sacrificial love of Jesus.

*Have participants read **Luke 22:14-23**.*

Discuss:

- Describe what must have been going through the disciples' minds as they broke bread with Jesus. What makes their experience different from our own when we celebrate the Lord's Supper?
- Describe what goes through your own mind as you celebrate the sacrament of Holy Communion. How is our experience with communion similar to that of the disciples?

Continue reading out loud:

> Let's also discuss the **Sacrament of Last Rites**: an anointing of the very ill or dying person of the Christian faith that includes remembrance of baptismal vows, confession, the Lord's Prayer, and Holy Communion. This serves to remind us of our lifelong walk with the Lord and proclaims our faith in salvation and eternal life.

*Have participants read **James 5:14-16** and **John 6:37-40**.*

Discuss:

- Have you ever witnessed a family member receive Last Rites, or have you received them yourself?
- Why do you think the sacrament of Last Rites is an important function of the church?

Bible Study and Discussion (15 mins.)

Read the following to the group:

> You are a people holy to the LORD your God. Out of all the peoples on the face of the earth, the LORD has chosen you to be his treasured possession.
>
> *(Deuteronomy 14:2)*

From the moment Adam and Eve fled Eden, God pursued the children he desperately loved. Throughout the centuries, he went behind them, went before them, and drew alongside them, calling them back into relationship with him. Calling them into covenant—a binding relationship that will last forever, just as it was always meant to be. This is why the children of Israel love Zion. God chose to make his dwelling place there with them. In Zion, they were a people set apart—to be the holy people of a holy God. And through the grace of our Lord Jesus Christ, we, as Gentiles, are included in this family of people who have been set apart. As the apostle Paul said in Ephesians 3:6, "This mystery is that through the gospel the Gentiles are heirs together with Israel, members together of one body, and sharers together in the promise in Christ Jesus."

From Mount Moriah, to Sinai and Carmel, and from the Mount of Beatitudes to Mount Tabor, God has called aside his people to teach them the attributes of holy living. And as we join our Hebrew brothers and sisters on Mount Zion, we are called to reflect the characteristics of the Holy One who walked among us—Jesus the Messiah.

Discuss:

Ask volunteers to read the following three Scriptures. After the readings, use a large sheet of paper (or chalkboard or dry erase board if available) to list the attributes of people who have been set apart for holy living. Participants should use insights from Scripture readings and past sessions.

- 1 Peter 1:14-16
- Colossians 3:1-17
- Philippians 2:14-16

Read the following to the group:

> *"And I tell you that you are Peter, and on this rock I will build my church, and the gates of Hades will not overcome it."*
>
> *(Matthew 16:18)*

The great Temple in Jerusalem was destroyed by the Roman Emperor Titus in AD 70. But it wasn't destroyed completely. A portion of the Temple's platform, now known as the Western Wall, still stands and is revered greatly by the people of Israel. Foremost in their hopes and prayers is that the Temple will one day be rebuilt. To visit this place is a remarkably moving experience. People from around the world come to stand before the Western Wall to enter into intensely private moments of worship. Millions of hands are laid against the now-smooth surface of the wall, making a physical connection with the roots of their faith. Millions of prayers are whispered or written lovingly and tucked into the crevices of the wall's massive stones. If the stones could speak the prayers they contain, they would speak well into eternity. Millions of tears soak the surface of the wall as cheeks of young and old are pressed upon the stones—as if pressing into the very being of God. Waiting . . . hoping . . . praying.

The ancient stones of the Western Wall have more of a story to tell. The sandaled feet of the Messiah once walked within their boundaries. His hands and cheeks once pressed up against them in prayer. And, during his brief earthly ministry, the Architect of a *new* Temple laid its foundation stone.

Have participants read the following Scriptures out loud:

- Isaiah 28:16
- Psalm 118:22-23
- 1 Corinthians 3:10-11, 16

Discuss:

- What foundation did Jesus lay during his earthly ministry? What was he building?
- In the construction of a building, stones are placed upon the foundational cornerstone. Each stone is unique as it arrives from the quarry and is then chiseled and sawed in order to fit perfectly with the other stones.

Have participants read the following Scriptures out loud:

- 1 Peter 2:4-5
- Ephesians 2:19-22
- Romans 12:3-8

Discuss:

- Peter describes the people of God as "living stones." Based on the three Scripture readings, describe the function of a living stone. What are we building?
- How is your individuality important in the body of believers?
- How is your ability to fit together with other believers important to the body of the church?

Session Closing (10 mins.*)

1. ***Peak Perspectives devotional:*** Ask participants to share insights they have journaled form the comparison given between Mount Zion and Mount Hermon.
2. ***Response to the foundational Scripture:*** Have participants turn to the lyrics of the song "The Holy City," found at the end of chapter 6 in the *Mountaintop Moments* book. In unison, read the lyrics out loud together.[1]
3. ***To close this final session of Mountaintop Moments:*** Celebrate the sacrament of Holy Communion together.[2]

*Class time will need to be adjusted to accommodate the service of Holy Communion.

Handout #1

The Beatitudes

(NIV)

"Blessed are the poor in spirit,
*   for theirs is the kingdom of heaven.*
Blessed are those who mourn,
*   for they will be comforted.*
Blessed are the meek,
*   for they will inherit the earth.*
Blessed are those who hunger and thirst for righteousness,
*   for they will be filled.*
Blessed are the merciful,
*   for they will be shown mercy.*
Blessed are the pure in heart,
*   for they will see God.*
Blessed are the peacemakers,
*   for they will be called children of God.*
Blessed are those who are persecuted because of righteousness,
*   for theirs is the kingdom of heaven.*

"Blessed are you when people insult you, persecute you and falsely say all kinds of evil against you because of me. Rejoice and be glad, because great is your reward in heaven, for in the same way they persecuted the prophets who were before you."

(Matthew 5:3-12)

Handout #2

The Beatitudes

(The Message)

"You're blessed when you're at the end of your rope. With less of you there is more of God and his rule.

"You're blessed when you feel you've lost what is most dear to you. Only then can you be embraced by the One most dear to you.

"You're blessed when you're content with just who you are—no more, no less. That's the moment you find yourselves proud owners of everything that can't be bought.

"You're blessed when you've worked up a good appetite for God. He's food and drink in the best meal you'll ever eat.

"You're blessed when you care. At the moment of being 'care-full,' you find yourselves cared for.

"You're blessed when you get your inside world—your mind and heart—put right. Then you can see God in the outside world.

"You're blessed when you can show people how to cooperate instead of compete or fight. That's when you discover who you really are, and your place in God's family.

"You're blessed when your commitment to God provokes persecution. The persecution drives you even deeper into God's kingdom.

"Not only that—count yourselves blessed every time people put you down or throw you out or speak lies about you to discredit me. What it means is that the truth is too close for comfort and they are uncomfortable. You can be glad when that happens—give a cheer, even!—for though they don't like it, I do! And all heaven applauds. And know that you are in good company. My prophets and witnesses have always gotten into this kind of trouble."

(Matthew 5:3-12 MSG)

Handout #3

The Ten Commandments

God spoke all these words:

> *I am God, your God,*
> > *who brought you out of the land of Egypt,*
> > *out of a life of slavery.*

No other gods, only me.

No carved gods of any size, shape, or form of anything whatever, whether of things that fly or walk or swim. Don't bow down to them and don't serve them because I am God, your God, and I'm a most jealous God, punishing the children for any sins their parents pass on to them to the third, and yes, even to the fourth generation of those who hate me. But I'm unswervingly loyal to the thousands who love me and keep my commandments.

No using the name of God, your God, in curses or silly banter; God won't put up with the irreverent use of his name.

Observe the Sabbath day, to keep it holy. Work six days and do everything you need to do. But the seventh day is a Sabbath to God, your God. Don't do any work—not you, nor your son, nor your daughter, nor your servant, nor your maid, nor your animals, not even the foreign guest visiting in your town. For in six days God made Heaven, Earth, and sea, and everything in them; he rested on the seventh day. Therefore God blessed the Sabbath day; he set it apart as a holy day.

Honor your father and mother so that you'll live a long time in the land that God, your God, is giving you.

No murder.

No adultery.

No stealing.

No lies about your neighbor.

No lusting after your neighbor's house—or wife or servant or maid or ox or donkey. Don't set your heart on anything that is your neighbor's.

(Exodus 20:1-17 MSG)

NOTES

Session 1: Moriah: Mount of Provision
1 "Great Is Thy Faithfulness," words by Thomas O. Chisholm, 1923, *The United Methodist Hymnal* (Nashville: The United Methodist Publishing House, 1989), 140. If you'd like to show a video, I recommend searching for the official music video by the vocal group Veritas.

Session 2: Sinai: Mount of God's Law
1 "Amazing Grace," words by John Newton, 1779, *The United Methodist Hymnal* (Nashville: The United Methodist Publishing House, 1989), 378. If you'd like to show a video, I recommend searching for the official video for "Sweetest Song I Know" by Armor Music Ministry.

Session 3: Carmel: Mount of Decision
1 "Trust and Obey," words by John H. Sammis, 1887, *The United Methodist Hymnal* (Nashville: The United Methodist Publishing House, 1989), 467. If you'd like to show a video, I recommend searching online for the version of "Trust and Obey" sung by Kaoma Chende.

Session 4: Beatitudes: Mount of Blessings
1 "I Surrender All," words by J. W. Van Deventer, 1896, *The United Methodist Hymnal* (Nashville: The United Methodist Publishing

House, 1989), 354. If you'd like to show a video, I recommend searching for the version of this traditional hymn performed by Newsboys.

Session 5: Tabor: Mount of Transfiguration

1 Strong's 3339, s.v. "metamorphoo," BibleStudyTools.com, accessed May 15, 2019, https://www.biblestudytools.com/lexicons/greek/nas/metamorphoo.html.

2 "A Journey with Christ," Walk to Emmaus, Upper Room Ministries, accessed May 7, 2019, http://emmaus.upperroom.org/about.

3 "The Apostles' Creed, Traditional Version," *The United Methodist Hymnal* (Nashville: The United Methodist Publishing House, 1989), 881.

Session 6: Zion: Mount of God's Presence

1 If you would like to watch a video of "The Holy City," I recommend searching for the version by the London Philharmonic Choir.

2 "A Service of Word and Table II," *The United Methodist Hymnal* (Nashville: The United Methodist Publishing House, 1989), 12-15.

CPSIA information can be obtained
at www.ICGtesting.com
Printed in the USA
LVHW021916110619
620906LV00001B/1